BIG IDEA

ROCKS AND MINERALS

Judy Halpern

SERIES EDITORS

Jim Cummins • David Freeman • Yvonne Freeman
Les Asselstine • Catherine Little

PEARSON

Pearson Canada Inc.
26 Prince Andrew Place
Don Mills, ON M3C 2T8
Customer Service: 1-800-361-6128

Ru′bĭcon
www.rubiconpublishing.com

Associate Publisher: Cheryl Turner
Editor: Lauren Wing
Editorial Assistant: Vicky He
Creative Director: Jennifer Drew
Designers: Jen Harvey, Brandon Koepke

13 14 15 16 17 5 4 3 2 1

ISBN: 978-1-77058-729-8

Paper used in the production of this book is a natural, recyclable product made from wood grown in sustainable forests. The manufacturing process conforms to the environmental regulations of the country of origin.

We acknowledge the financial support of the Government of Canada through the Canada Book Fund for our publishing activities.

BIG IDEA

CONTENTS

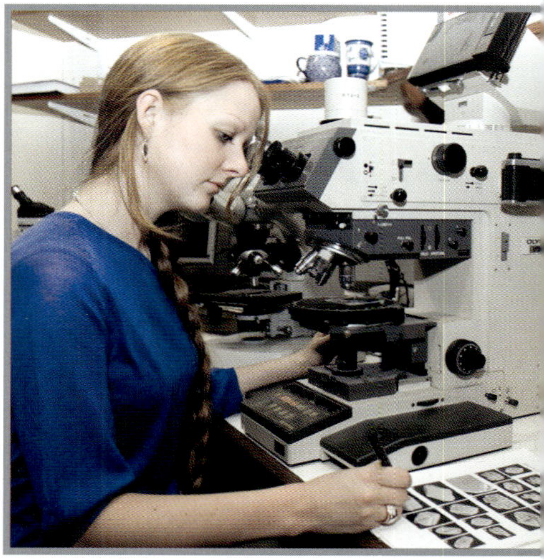

Exploring Rocks and Minerals

BIG IDEA People use rocks and minerals in many ways.

Minerals and rocks come from the ground.

Minerals are made of only one thing.

Rocks are made of two or more minerals.

How do we use rocks and minerals?

CHAPTER 1

ROCKS

There are three types of rocks. They all come from the ground.

1 IGNEOUS ROCK

Example: Pumice

2 SEDIMENTARY ROCK

Example: Sandstone

3 METAMORPHIC ROCK

Example: Marble

BIG IDEA People use rocks in many ways.

Some rocks are rough. Some rocks are soft. Some rocks are hard. People have found different ways to use rocks.

Pumice

Pumice is a rough rock.
It can be used to scrape things.
People use pumice to make their feet smooth.

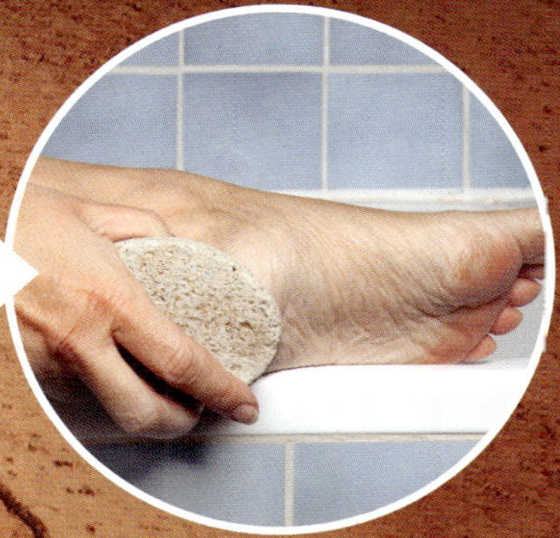

Sandstone

Sandstone is a soft rock.
It is easy to cut.
Sandstone can be used to make sculptures and statues.

Marble

Marble is a hard rock.
It can be used to make buildings.
People use marble to make floors and walls.

1. Why do people use pumice to make their feet smooth?
2. Why do people use marble in buildings?

Igneous Rock

BIG IDEA Hot liquid rock can change into igneous rock.

There is hot liquid rock inside Earth. Sometimes it comes out of the ground. It changes into igneous rock.

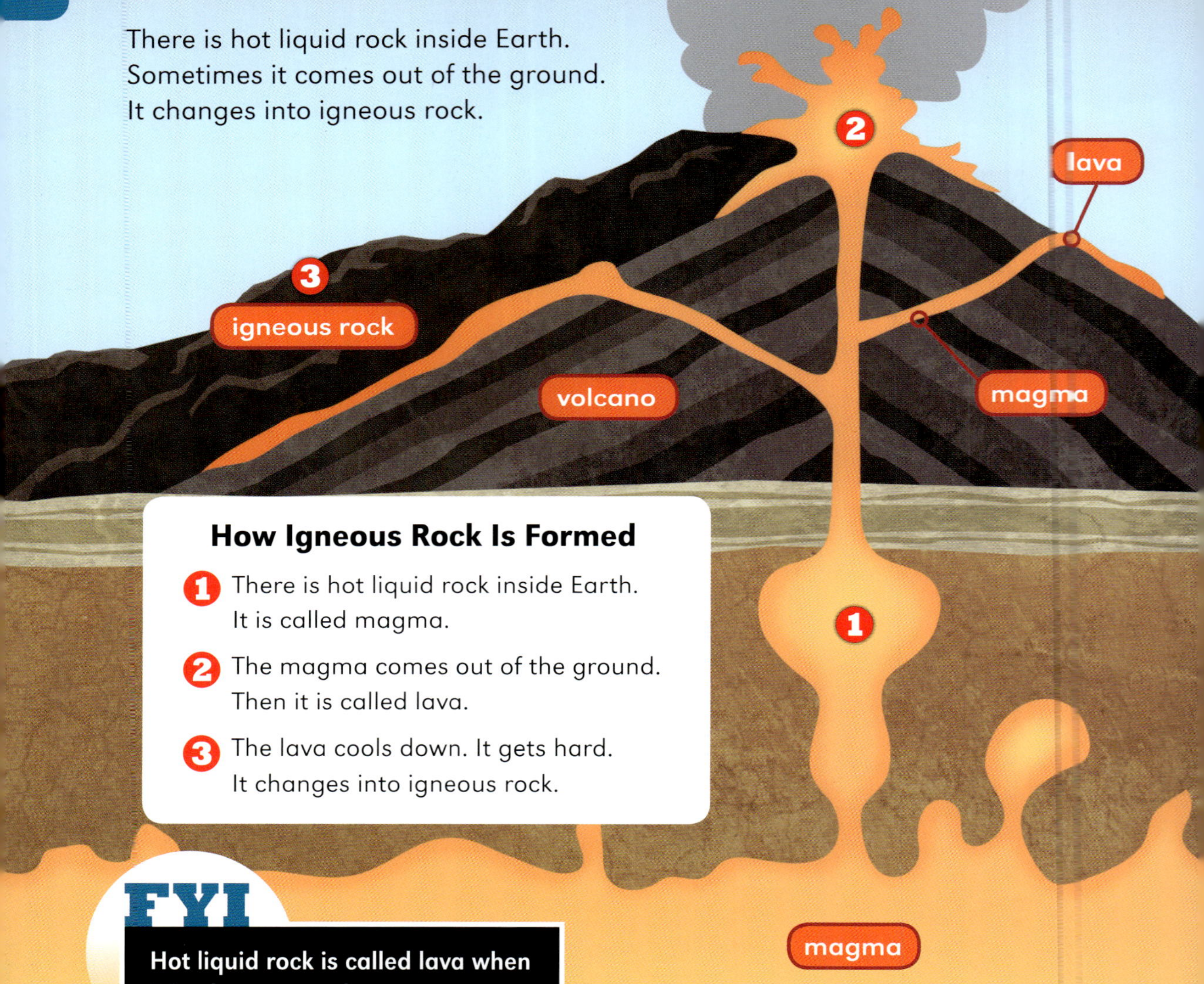

How Igneous Rock Is Formed

1. There is hot liquid rock inside Earth. It is called magma.
2. The magma comes out of the ground. Then it is called lava.
3. The lava cools down. It gets hard. It changes into igneous rock.

FYI

Hot liquid rock is called lava when it is above ground.

?

1. What does lava change into when it gets hard?
2. What could make lava cool down?

ACTIVITY 1

OBSERVE IGNEOUS ROCKS

Scientists can identify igneous rocks by looking at them. These igneous rocks look very different. They were formed in the same way. But they are made of different minerals.

1

2

3

4

5

Colour

Igneous rocks can be:

- white
- pink
- green
- black
- brown
- grey
- mix of colours

Texture

Igneous rocks can be:

- rough
- smooth

FYI

Sometimes you can see crystals in rocks. The crystals are minerals.

1. Make a chart. Record the colour of each rock.
2. Does each rock look rough or smooth? Record the texture of each rock.
3. Record other words to tell how the rocks look.

Rock	Colour	Texture (rough or smooth)	Other Words
#1			

ANALYZE & REFLECT

Why do the igneous rocks look different?

Sedimentary Rock

BIG IDEA Sedimentary rock has layers.

Rock, soil, and leaves sit on the bottom of lakes and oceans. Over a long time, they change into sedimentary rock.

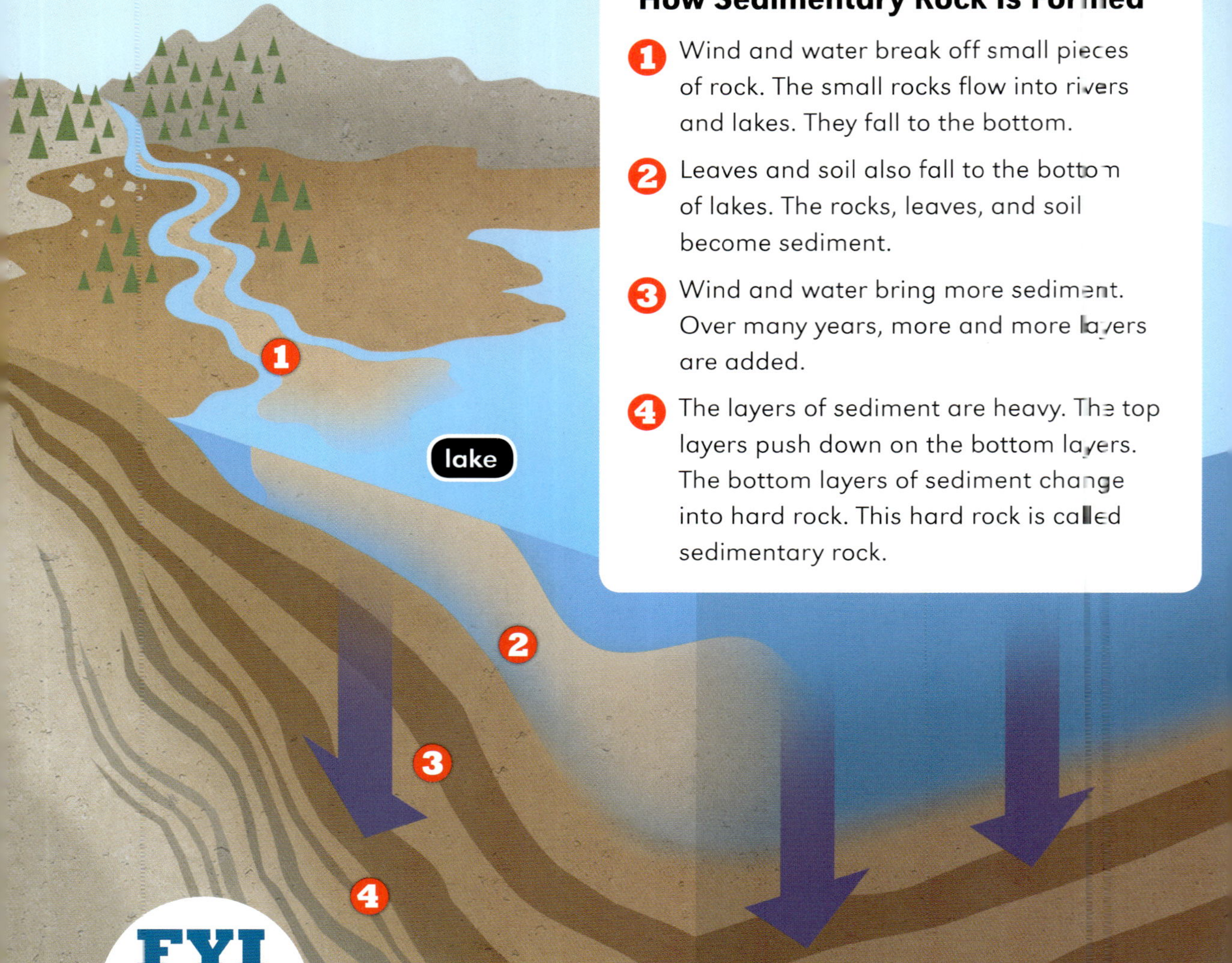

How Sedimentary Rock Is Formed

1. Wind and water break off small pieces of rock. The small rocks flow into rivers and lakes. They fall to the bottom.
2. Leaves and soil also fall to the bottom of lakes. The rocks, leaves, and soil become sediment.
3. Wind and water bring more sediment. Over many years, more and more layers are added.
4. The layers of sediment are heavy. The top layers push down on the bottom layers. The bottom layers of sediment change into hard rock. This hard rock is called sedimentary rock.

FYI

Limestone is a sedimentary rock. It is used to make cement, paint, and paper.

?

1. What changes into sedimentary rock?
2. How does sedimentary rock get layers?

ACTIVITY 2

OBSERVE SEDIMENTARY ROCKS

Scientists can identify sedimentary rocks by looking at them. These sedimentary rocks look very different. They were formed in the same way. But they are made of different minerals.

1

2

3

4

5

Colour

Sedimentary rocks can be:

- white
- pink
- green
- black
- brown
- grey
- mix of colours

Texture

Sedimentary rocks can be:

- rough
- smooth

Layers

Sedimentary rocks have layers.

FYI

Fossils are remains of plants or animals that died a long time ago. They are mostly found in sedimentary rock.

1 Make a chart. Record the colours of the rocks.

2 Record the texture of each rock.

3 Can you see layers in the rocks? Record your answer on your chart.

Rock	Colour	Texture (rough or smooth)	Can you see layers?
#1			

ANALYZE & REFLECT

How are sedimentary rocks different from igneous rocks?

Metamorphic Rock

BIG IDEA Igneous rock and sedimentary rock can change into metamorphic rock.

It is very hot deep inside Earth. The heat can change igneous rock and sedimentary rock.

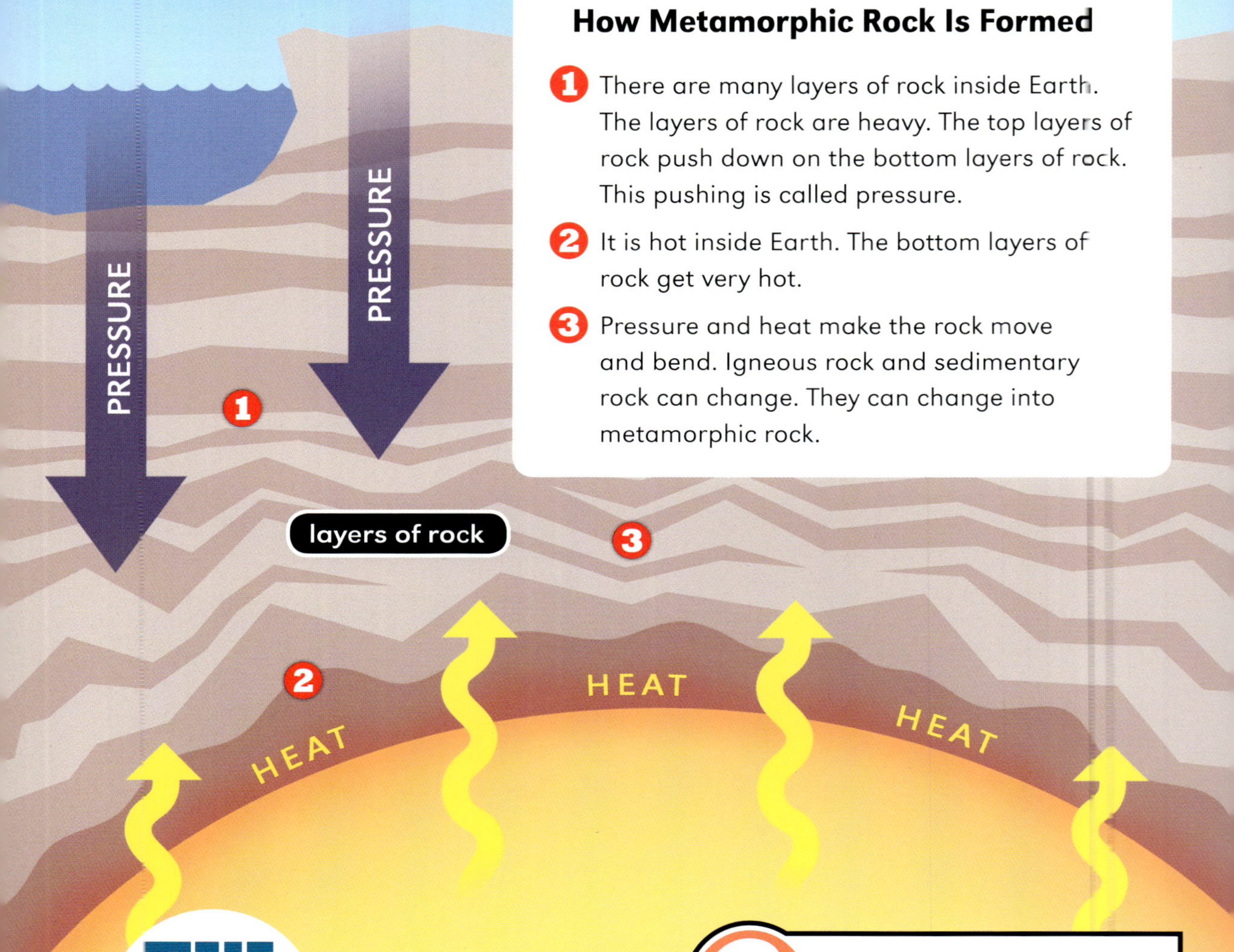

How Metamorphic Rock Is Formed

1. There are many layers of rock inside Earth. The layers of rock are heavy. The top layers of rock push down on the bottom layers of rock. This pushing is called pressure.
2. It is hot inside Earth. The bottom layers of rock get very hot.
3. Pressure and heat make the rock move and bend. Igneous rock and sedimentary rock can change. They can change into metamorphic rock.

FYI

Soapstone is a metamorphic rock. It is used to make sinks and kitchen counters.

soapstone sink

?

1. What can change into metamorphic rock?
2. What makes pressure inside Earth?
3. How do pressure and heat make rocks change?

ACTIVITY 3

OBSERVE METAMORPHIC ROCKS

Scientists can identify metamorphic rocks by looking at them. These metamorphic rocks look very different. They were formed in the same way. But they are made of different minerals.

1

2

3

4

5

Colour

Metamorphic rocks can be:

- white
- red
- black
- brown
- grey
- green
- mix of colours

Texture

Metamorphic rocks are usually smooth.

Lines

Metamorphic rocks may have lines.

1 Make a chart. Record the colours of the rocks.

2 Record the texture of each rock.

3 Can you see lines in the rocks? Record your answer on your chart.

Rock	Colour	Texture (rough or smooth)	Lines (yes or no)
#1			

ANALYZE & REFLECT

1. How are metamorphic rocks different from igneous rocks?
2. How are metamorphic rocks different from sedimentary rocks?

CHAPTER 2

MINERALS

People use minerals every day.
What minerals do you use?

BIG IDEA People use minerals in many different ways.

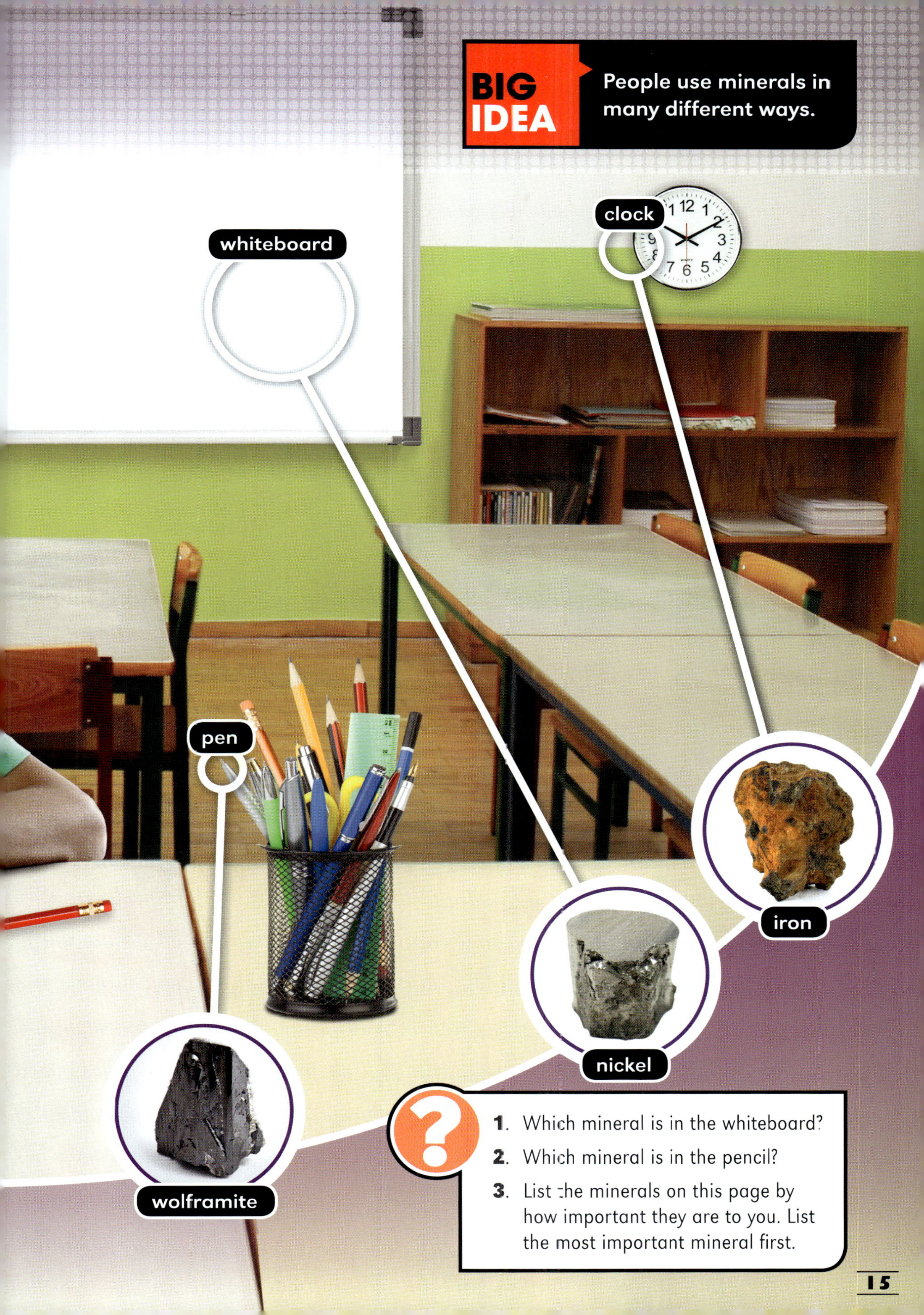

1. Which mineral is in the whiteboard?
2. Which mineral is in the pencil?
3. List the minerals on this page by how important they are to you. List the most important mineral first.

Looking at Minerals

BIG IDEA We can identify minerals by looking at them.

Some scientists study minerals.
These scientists are called geologists.

Geologists identify minerals.
They study the properties of the minerals.
A property is how something looks or acts.

Property: Lustre

Some materials are very shiny. Some materials are dull.
The word lustre is used to describe how shiny a material is.
Lustre can be used to identify minerals.

Glassy Glassy minerals look clear like glass.

Metallic Metallic minerals look shiny.

Silky Silky minerals look smooth like silk.

Waxy Waxy minerals look like wax.

Dull Dull minerals do not shine.

Property: Colour

Colour can be used to identify minerals.

Red

Orange

Yellow

Green

Blue

Purple

Property: Transparency

Light goes through some materials. That means they are transparent. Transparency can be used to identify minerals.

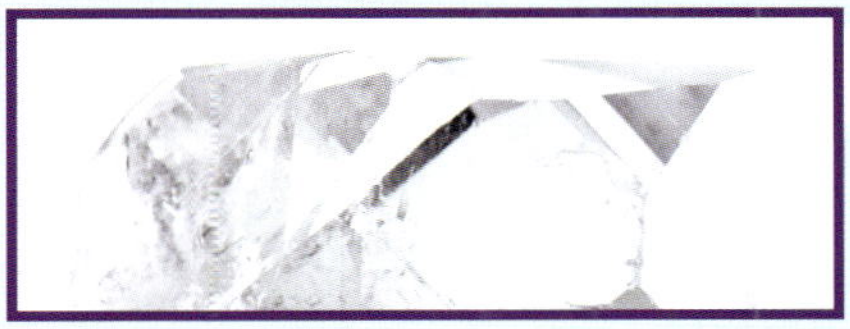

Transparent Light goes through it. We can also see through it.

Translucent Some light goes through it. We cannot see through it clearly.

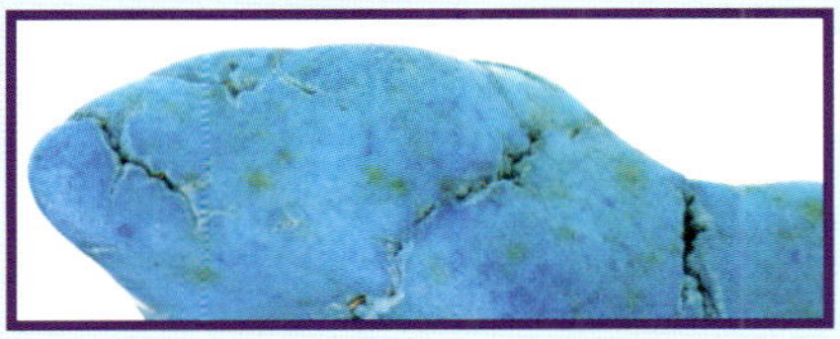

Opaque Light does not go through it. We cannot see through it.

FYI

Geologists test minerals by hitting them with a hammer. They test to see what happens when the mineral breaks.

?

1. What properties can be used to describe minerals?
2. Which property is easy to see? Why?

Testing Minerals

BIG IDEA We can identify minerals by doing tests.

Some minerals look like another mineral. Tests can be done to identify minerals.

TEST: Hardness — Scratch Test

Some minerals are hard. Some minerals are soft.

The hardness test shows which minerals are hard. It also shows which minerals are soft.

The minerals are scratched with different objects.

Soft minerals are easy to scratch.

Hardness is measured on a scale of 1 to 10. Soft minerals are a 1. Hard minerals are a 10.

TEST: Colour — Streak Test

A mineral can be identified by colour.
A test can also be done for colour.

The mineral is rubbed on a hard surface.
The mineral makes a mark. The mark is called a streak.
The streak shows the mineral's true colour.

Hematite looks black.
But its true colour is dark red.

Hematite is used to make
the red in some red paint.

TEST: Magnetism — Magnet Test

A mineral can be tested with a magnet.
A mineral that sticks to a magnet is magnetic.

Magnetite is the most magnetic mineral.

1. Is talc a soft mineral or a hard mineral?
2. Which test shows a mineral's true colour?

ACTIVITY 4 DO A MAGNET TEST

Find out if minerals are magnetic.

YOU WILL NEED

minerals

magnet

pencil and paper

1 Hold the magnet beside the mineral. You might feel the magnet pull toward the mineral. This means the mineral is magnetic.

2 Make a chart. Record your results.

Mineral	Magnetic (yes or no)
Magnetite	Yes

3 Test the other minerals.

ANALYZE & REFLECT

1. Which is the most magnetic mineral you tested?
2. Why do geologists do a magnet test?

ACTIVITY 5

DO A SCRATCH TEST

Test how hard minerals are.

YOU WILL NEED

minerals

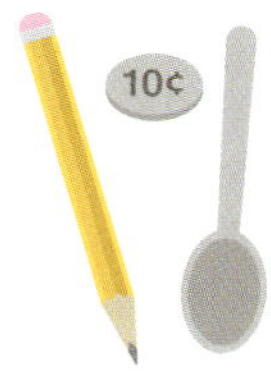

scratch tools

safety glasses

pencil and paper

1 Put on safety glasses.

2 Try to scratch one mineral with the pencil.
Record your results.

3 Try to scratch the mineral with the other scratch tools. Record your results on a chart.
Write "no" if the tool did not scratch the mineral.
Write "yes" if the tool did scratch the mineral.
Stop testing when you see a small scratch.

4 Record a hardness number for the mineral.

5 Test the other minerals.
Record your results.

SCRATCH TOOL HARDNESS SCALE

Scratch Tools	Hardness
sharp pencil	1.5
fingernail	2.5
dime	3.0
spoon	5.5

Mineral	Sharp Pencil	Fingernail	Dime	Spoon	Hardness
gypsum	no	yes	→	→	2.5

The scratch test will help you compare the hardness of the minerals.
But it does not give an exact number.

BE SAFE

Wear safety glasses when you do the scratch test.

ANALYZE & REFLECT

1. Which mineral is the hardest?
Which mineral is the softest?
2. How did you decide what number to give the minerals?

CHAPTER 3

MINING ROCKS AND MI

FYI

A mine is a hole dug in the ground to get rocks or minerals. A person who works in a mine is called a miner.

NERALS

BIG IDEA People get rocks and minerals out of the ground to use them. This is called mining.

salt mine
Ontario

diamond mine
Northwest Territories

1. What is mined in Nunavut?
2. List three words to describe the mines in the pictures.
3. What is the hardest thing about mining? Discuss your ideas with a classmate.

Types of Mines

BIG IDEA There are two types of mines: surface mines and underground mines.

Surface Mines

Some rocks and minerals are close to the surface of the ground. People dig surface mines to get these minerals.

1. Machines scrape off the top layers of soil.
2. The miners collect the rocks and minerals.

Surface mines can be used to mine:

coal

gold

diamonds

FYI

Mining companies must plan how they will fix the land after a mine is closed. The Butchart Gardens in Victoria, British Columbia, was planted on top of an old surface mine.

Underground Mines

Some rocks and minerals are deep under the ground. People dig underground mines to get these rocks and minerals.

Underground mines can be dangerous to work in. They can be hot. The tunnels can collapse. There can be poisonous gases.

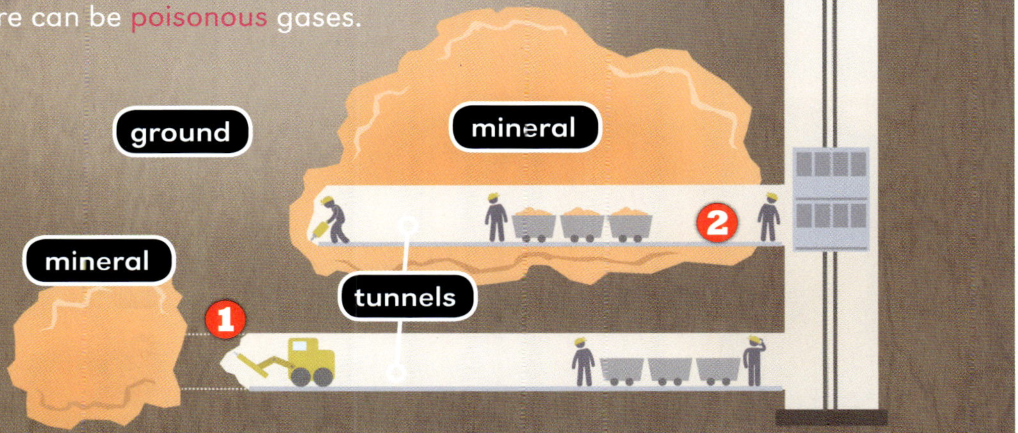

1. Machines dig tunnels under the ground.
2. The miners collect the rocks and minerals.

Underground mines can be used to mine:

1. When are surface mines used?
2. Why are underground mines dangerous?
3. Mines change the land. Do you think that is okay? Should people keep digging mines? Why?

Mining Changes Lives

BIG IDEA **We need mines to get rocks and minerals. But mines can cause problems.**

We use rocks and minerals in many different ways. But we have to get them out of the ground so we can use them.

Mining gives people jobs.

We mine coal. It can be burned to make electricity.

Mining gives us materials for building roads, ramps, and buildings.

Mining changes the land. The changes can harm plants and animals.

Mining can cause pollution of the air, land, and water.

Mining can be dangerous for miners.

1. Why do we need mines?
2. What is the biggest problem caused by mines? Give a reason for your answer.
3. Do you think people should stop mining? Why?

ACTIVITY 6

READ A MINING MAP

There are many mines in Canada. This map shows some of the mines. Read the map. Find the mines.

Where do I live?	What is mined where I live?	Rock or Mineral?	What do we make with it?	Do I use it? How?
Nova Scotia	zinc	mineral	sunscreen	I use sunscreen at the beach. It stops my skin from getting burned by the sun.

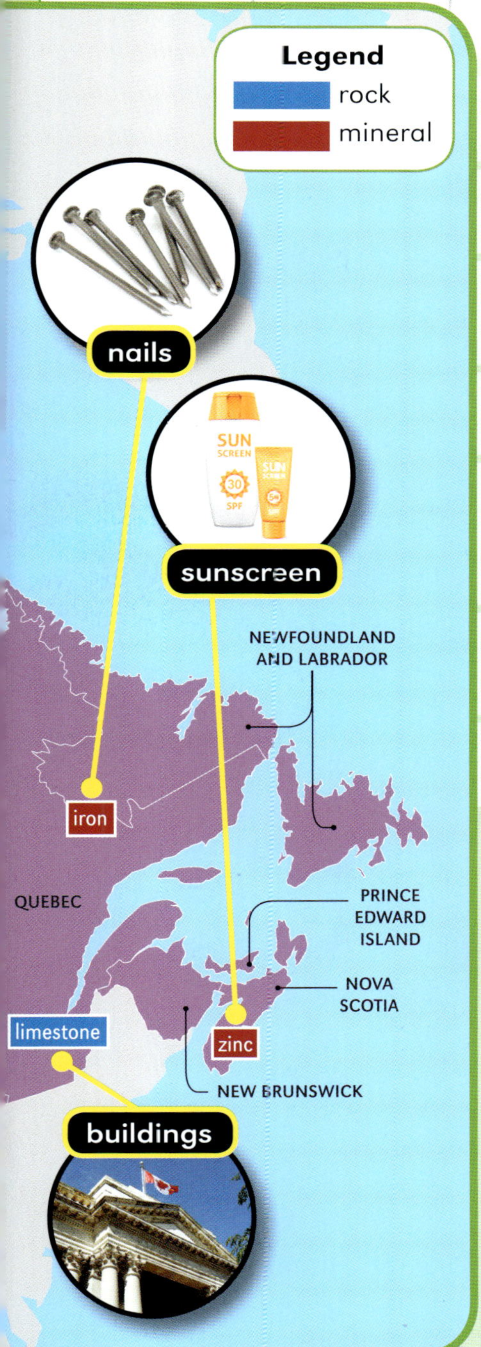

1 Make a chart like the one above.

2 Find where you live on the map.

3 Find a mine close to where you live. Record the rock or mineral mined.

4 Record what the rock or mineral is used to make.

5 Do you use something made from the rock or mineral? Write a short sentence to tell how you use it.

6 Read about the other mines in Canada. Add other rocks or minerals you use to your chart.

7 Find out about other mines close to where you live.

ANALYZE & REFLECT

1. Which rocks and minerals do you use most? Where are they mined?
2. How important are the rocks and minerals mined in Canada? How important is it to protect the air, land, and water? Which is more important? Why?

THINK LIKE AN INVENTOR

TO REUSE ROCKS AND MINERALS

Many things are made from rocks and minerals.
Cans and glass jars are made from rocks and minerals.

What can we do with cans and glass jars after we use them?

Cans and glass jars can be **recycled**. Cans and glass jars can also be reused. Reusing is better than recycling. Energy is not used to melt the cans and glass jars.

Invent a new way to use something made from a rock or a mineral.

1 Choose an object that is made from a rock or mineral.
Here are some ideas:

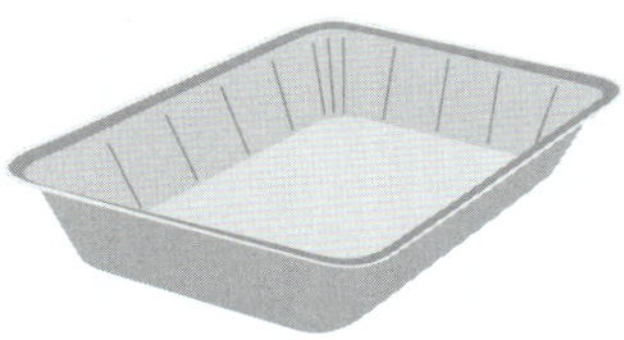

metal tray

glass jar

metal can

pop can

2 Invent a new way to use the object.
Some ideas are:

- pencil holder
- snow globe
- musical instrument

Be creative!

3 Draw a plan for making your invention.

4 Make your invention.

5 Test your invention. Find ways to make it better.

COMMUNICATE

1 Present your invention to the class. Describe how your invention works. Tell what you reused in your invention. Tell what rocks or minerals are in your invention.

2 Draw instructions for making your invention.

3 Ask a classmate to test your invention. Ask your classmate how you can make your invention better.

VOCABULARY

1 Find the words "igneous," "sedimentary," and "metamorphic" in this book. Draw a picture for each word. Write a definition for each word. Write an important point to remember for each word.

Word	Drawing	Definition	Important Point
Igneous			

2 Many words in this book have opposites. One example is rough/smooth. Find five words that have opposites. Compare your words with a classmate's words.

REVIEW

Talk about these questions with a classmate.

1. How are rocks different from minerals?
2. List three ways we use rocks.
3. How are igneous rocks made?
4. What three tests can we use to identify minerals?
5. What are the two types of mining?
6. What are two good things about mining?
7. What are two bad things about mining?
8. What rocks and minerals do you reuse?

Glossary

collapse (kuh-laps)	fall down
formed (formd)	made over time
identify (i-den-tuh-fi)	find out what something is
invent (in-vent)	create something for the first time
liquid (lih-kwid)	a substance that flows, such as water
poisonous (poy-zuhn-us)	causes sickness or death in living things
pollution (puh-loo-shun)	something that makes the land, air, or water harmful to people and other living things
recycled (ree-si-kuhld)	made a used material into something else
scale (skale)	a list of numbers used to measure something — for example, hardness — from soft (1) to hard (10)
surface (sur-fis)	the top part of something

Index